UKULELE

TOP HITS OF 2016

ISBN 978-1-4950-7255-0

HAL•LEONARD®
7777 W. BLUEMOUND RD. P.O. BOX 13819 MILWAUKEE, WI 53213

Visit Hal Leonard Online at
www.halleonard.com

Cake by the Ocean

Words and Music by Joseph Jonas, Justin Tranter, Robin Fredriksson and Mattias Larsson

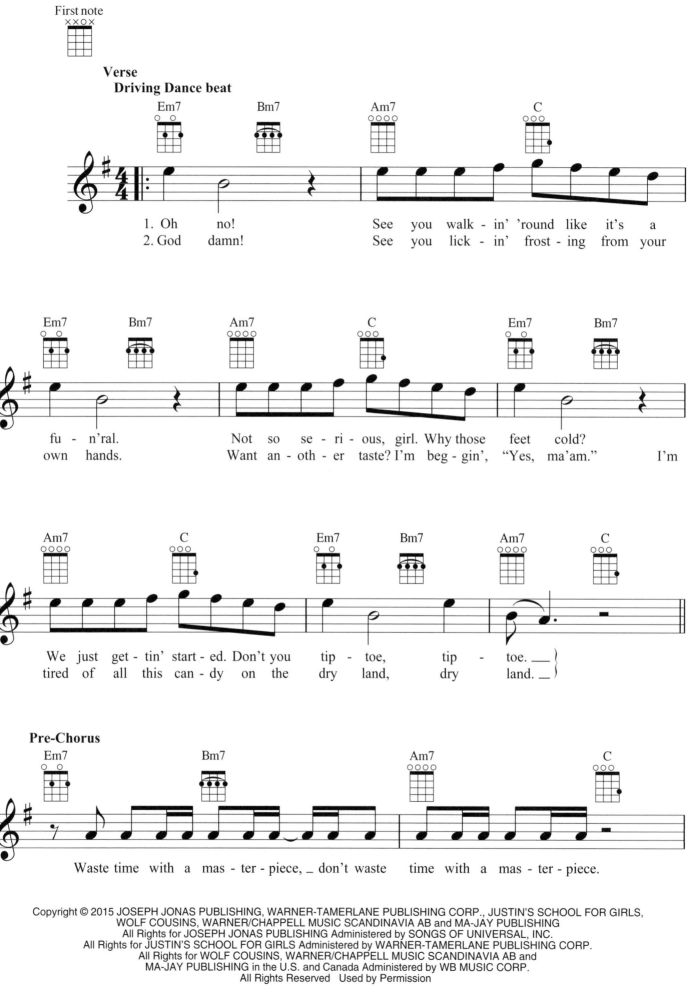

You should be roll-in' with me, ___ you should be roll-in' with me, ah. ___

You're a real-life fan-ta-sy, ___ you're a real-life fan-ta-sy.

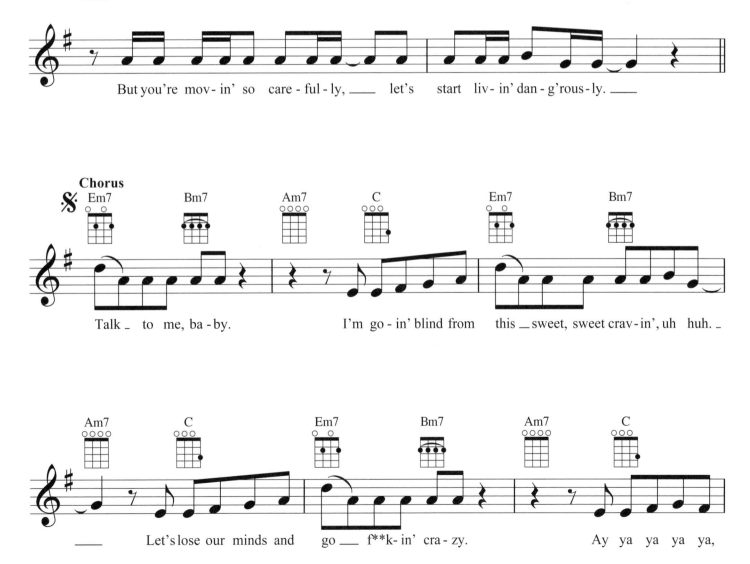

N.C.

But you're mov-in' so care-ful-ly, ___ let's start liv-in' dan-g'rous-ly. ___

Chorus

Talk _ to me, ba-by. I'm go-in' blind from this _ sweet, sweet crav-in', uh huh. _

___ Let's lose our minds and go ___ f**k-in' cra-zy. Ay ya ya ya ya,

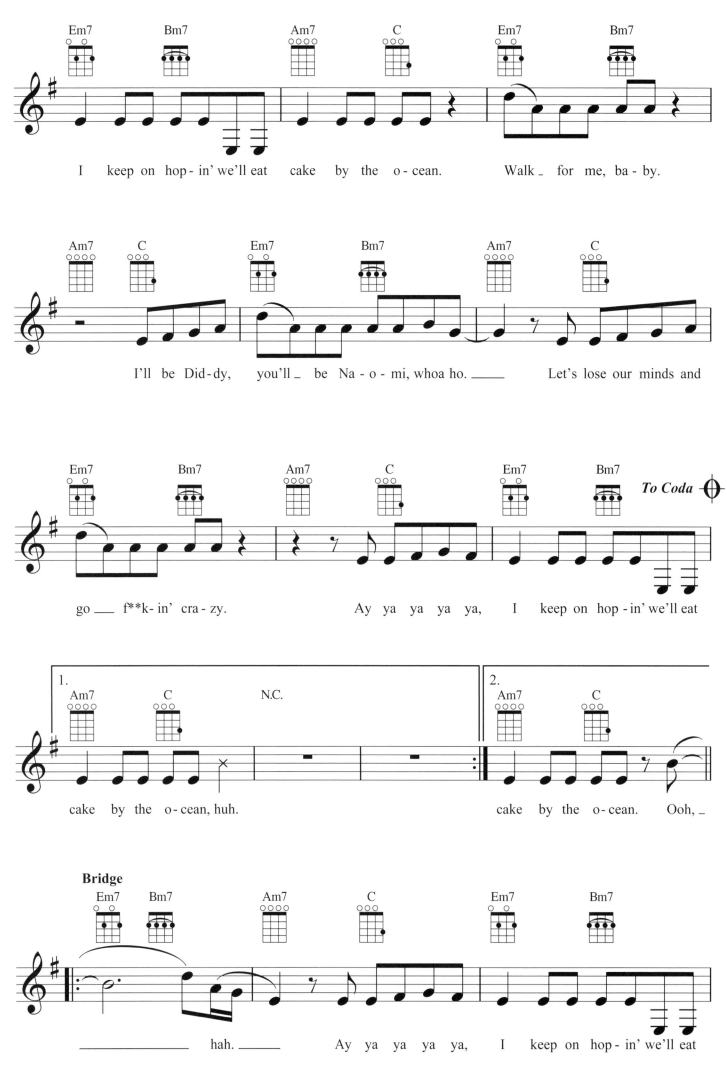

Can't Stop the Feeling

from TROLLS

Words and Music by Justin Timberlake, Max Martin and Shellback

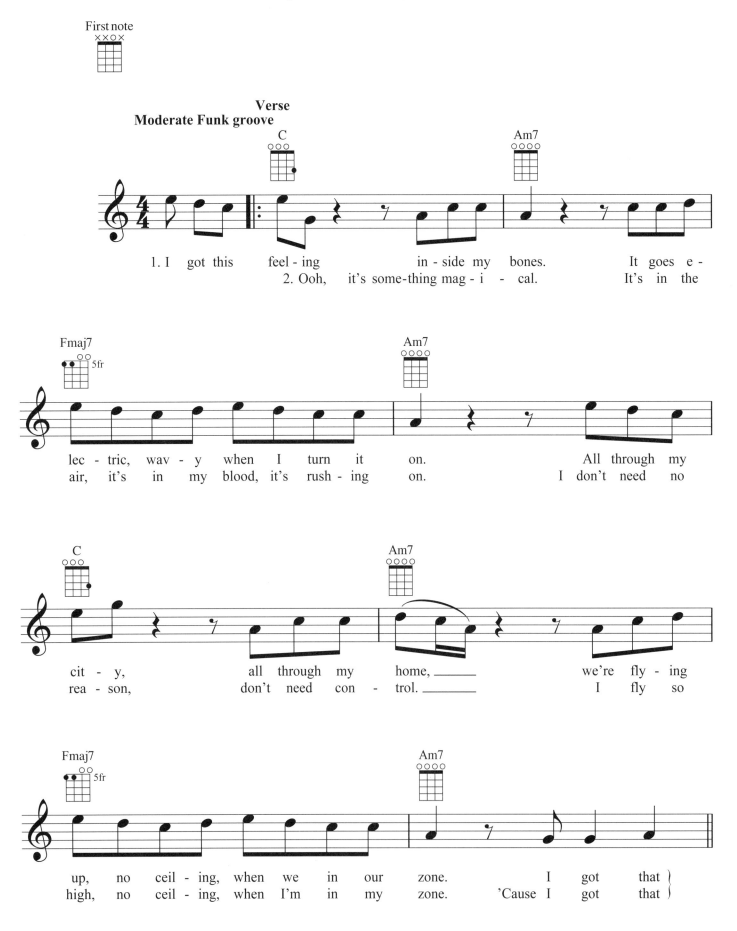

well, you al - read - y know. So just i - mag -

- ine, (just i - mag - ine,) (just i - mag - ine.)

Chorus

Noth - ing I can see but you when you dance, dance, dance. I feel - a good,

good creep - ing up on you, so just dance, dance, dance. Come on!

All those things I should - n't do, but you dance, dance, dance. And ain't

no - bod - y leav - ing soon, so keep danc - ing. I can't stop the feel -

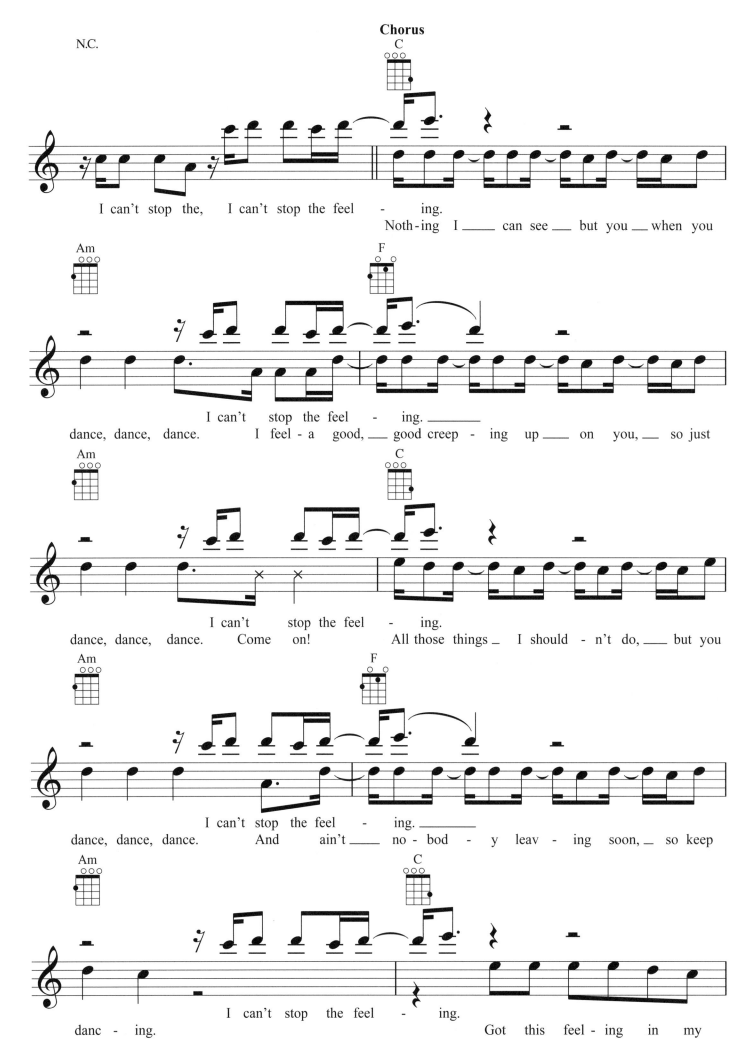

Cheap Thrills

Words and Music by Sia Furler, Greg Kurstin and Sean Paul Henriques

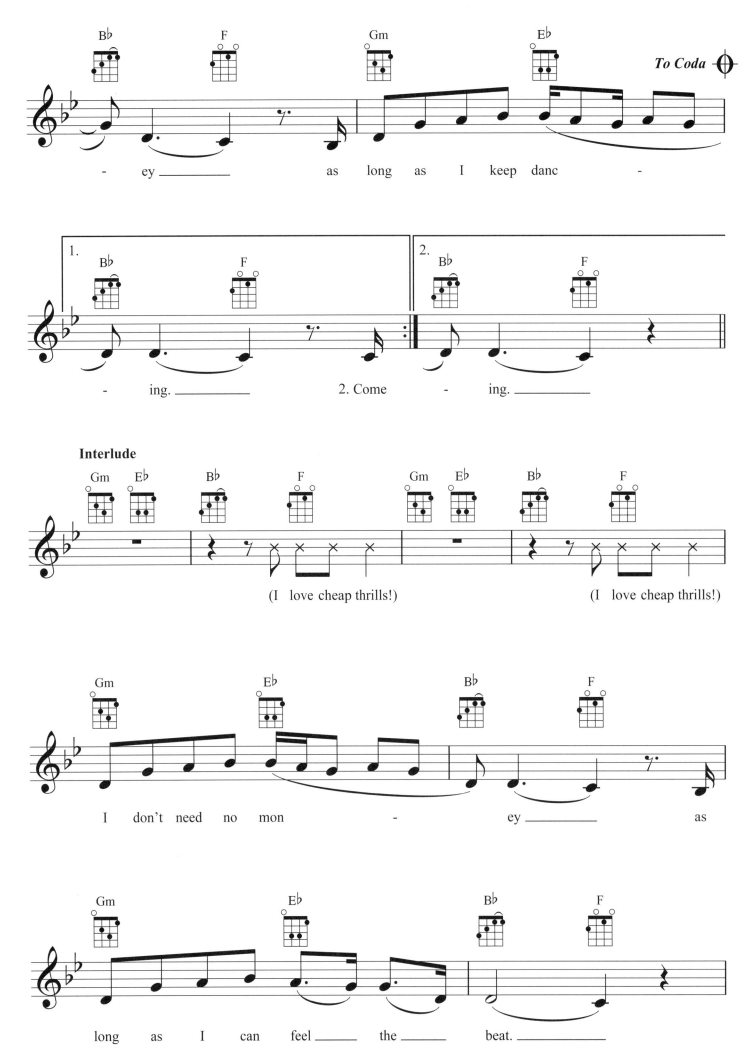

To Coda

- ey _____ as long as I keep danc -

1. - ing. _____ 2. Come - ing. _____

Interlude

(I love cheap thrills!) (I love cheap thrills!)

I don't need no mon - ey _____ as

long as I can feel _____ the _____ beat. _____

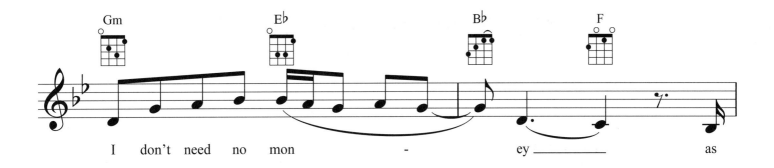

I don't need no mon - ey _____ as

D.S. al Coda

(Oh, oh.)

long as I keep danc - ing. Ba - by,

Outro

- ing. _____ La la la la la la la.

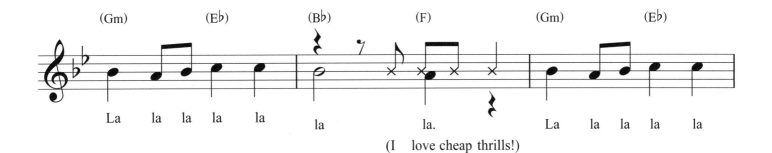

La la la la la la la.
(I love cheap thrills!)
La la la la la

la la.
(I love cheap thrills!)
La la la la la la la.
(I love cheap thrills!)

Hold Back the River

Words and Music by James Bay and Iain Archer

(1.,2.) see where you __ hide.
(3.) be by your __ side.

Hold ____ back the riv-er, hold ____ back. __ Hold __

Interlude

____ back. __ Oh, oh, oh, _____ oh, oh. _____

Oh, oh, _____ oh. _____

Bridge

sing 8va on repeat

____ Lone - ly ____ wa - ter,

lone - ly ____ wa - ter, won't __ you let us ____ wan -

- der, let us ____ hold ____ each oth - er?

D.S. al Coda 2
(with repeat)

2. Gm

(sing at written pitch)

let us ____ hold _____ each oth - er? Hold_

Coda 2

C

be by your _ side. Hold ____ back the riv - er, hold. ____

Bridge

F

Lone - ly ____ wa - ter, lone - ly ____ wa - ter, won't _ you

B♭

let us ____ wan - der,

1. Gm

let us ____ hold ____ each oth - er?

2. Gm

let us ____ hold ____ each oth - er?

Outro

Dm   C   F   B♭

(Instrumental)

F   B♭   F   C5

I Took a Pill in Ibiza

Words and Music by Mike Posner

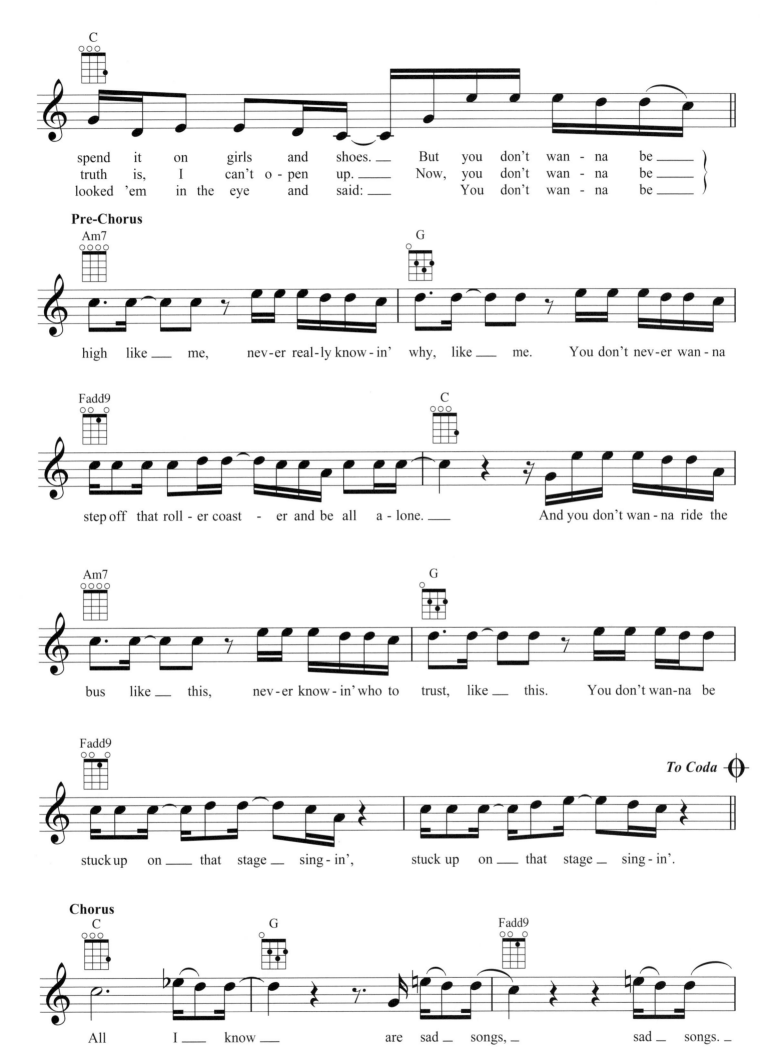

spend it on girls and shoes. ___ But you don't wan-na be ___
truth is, I can't o-pen up. ___ Now, you don't wan-na be ___
looked 'em in the eye and said: ___ You don't wan-na be ___

Pre-Chorus

high like ___ me, nev-er real-ly know-in' why, like ___ me. You don't nev-er wan-na

step off that roll-er coast ___ er and be all a-lone. ___ And you don't wan-na ride the

bus like ___ this, nev-er know-in' who to trust, like ___ this. You don't wan-na be

To Coda

stuck up on ___ that stage ___ sing-in', stuck up on ___ that stage ___ sing-in'.

Chorus

All I ___ know ___ are sad ___ songs, ___ sad ___ songs. ___

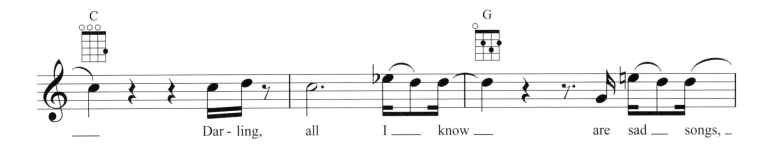

Dar - ling, all I ___ know ___ are sad ___ songs, ___

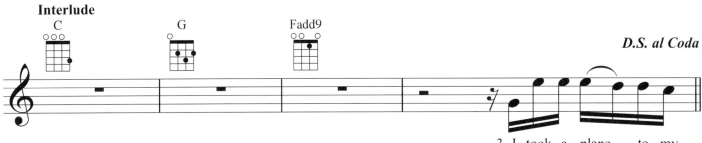

sad ___ songs. ___   2. I'm just a ___

Interlude

D.S. al Coda

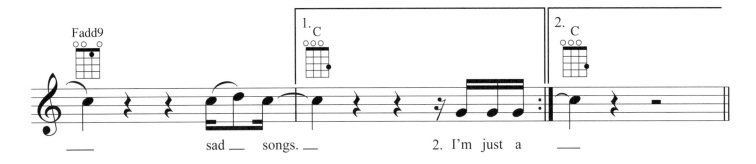

3. I took a plane ___ to my

Outro-Chorus

Coda

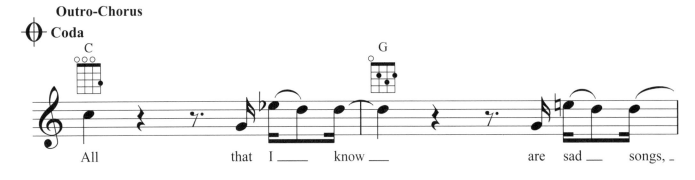

All that I ___ know ___ are sad ___ songs, ___

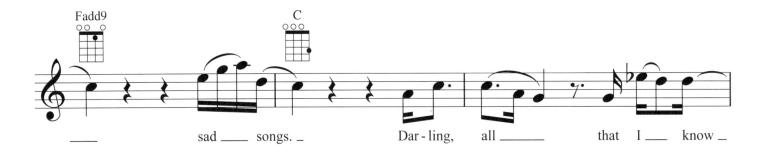

___ sad ___ songs. ___   Dar - ling, all ___ that I ___ know ___

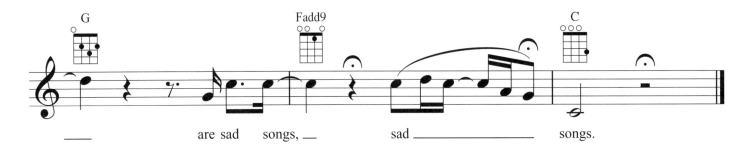

___ are sad songs, ___ sad ___ songs.

H.O.L.Y.

Words and Music by busbee, Nate Cyphert and William Wiik Larsen

I nev - er meant to cry, _____ start - ed los - in' hope. _____
get you sing - in', babe, _____ hal - le - lu -

But some-how, _ ba - by, you broke through and saved _ me. } You're an an -
- jah. _____ We'll be touch - in', we'll be touch - in' heav - en. }

Pre-Chorus

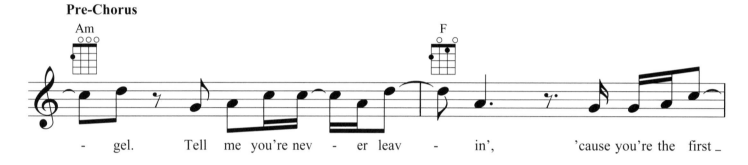

- gel. Tell me you're nev - er leav - in', 'cause you're the first _

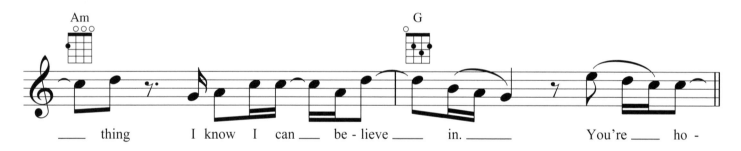

_____ thing I know I can _ be - lieve _____ in. _____ You're _____ ho -

Chorus

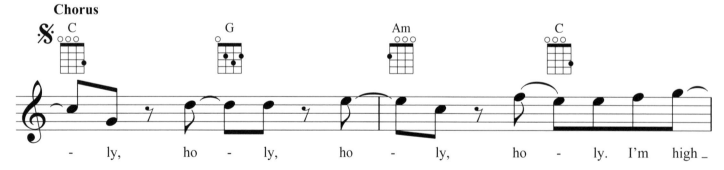

- ly, ho - ly, ho - ly, ho - ly. I'm high _

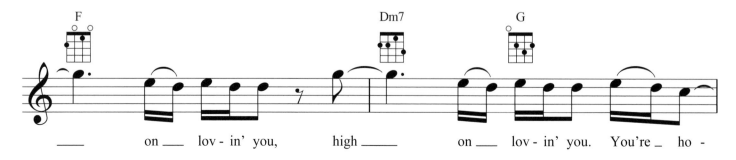

_____ on _ lov - in' you, high _____ on _ lov - in' you. You're _ ho -

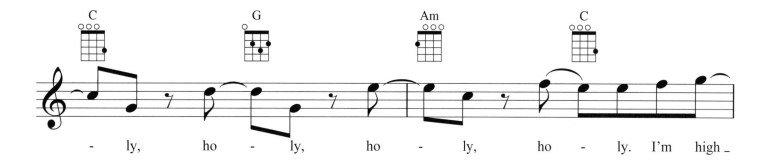

-ly, ho - ly, ho - ly, ho - ly. I'm high __

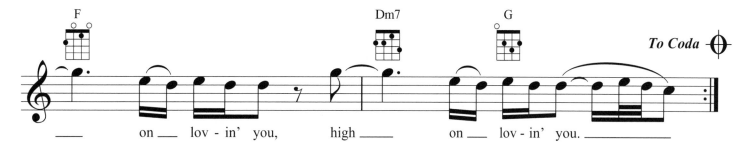

___ on __ lov - in' you, high ___ on __ lov - in' you. ___

Bridge

I don't need these stars, 'cause you shine for me.

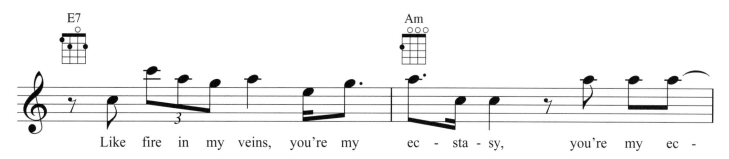

Like fire in my veins, you're my ec - sta - sy, you're my ec -

D.S. al Coda
(no repeat)

Outro Coda

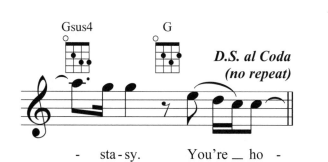

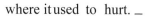

- sta - sy. You're __ ho -   You're the heal - in' hands __ where it used to hurt. __

rit.

You're my sav - in' grace, __ you're my kind of church. ___ You're __ ho - ly. __

Just Like Fire

from ALICE THROUGH THE LOOKING GLASS (WDP)

Words and Music by Alecia Moore, Max Martin, Shellback and Oscar Holter

* Vocal sung an octave lower than written.

E - ven when I give it all a - way, I want it all, ____ mm. ____ } (We came here to
We don't have to wor-ry 'bout a thing, a-bout a thing, ___ no. ____

Pre-Chorus

run it, run it, run it. We came here to run it, run it,

N.C.

Chorus

run it.) Just like fi - re, burn-in' up the way, if I can light the

world up for just one day, watch this mad-ness, col-or-ful cha-rade. No one can

be just like me an-y-way. Just like mag-ic, I'll be fly-in' free. I'm-a dis-ap-

** Vocal sung at written pitch.

* *Vocal sung an octave lower than written.*

_____ what's a girl to do? _____ Mm, _____ what's a girl to do? _____ Just like

Chorus

fi - re, burn - in' up the way, if I can light the world up for just one day, _ watch this

D.S. al Coda
(take 2nd ending)

mad - ness, col - or - ful cha - rade. No one can be just like me an - y - way. Just like

run it. We came here to run it, run it, run it.)
Just like fi - re.

Additional Lyrics

Rap: So look, I came here to run it, just 'cause nobody's done it.
Y'all don't think I could run it, but look, I've been here, I've done it.
Impossible? Please! Watch, I do it with ease.
You just gotta believe. Come on, come on with me.

Lost Boy

Words and Music by Ruth Berhe

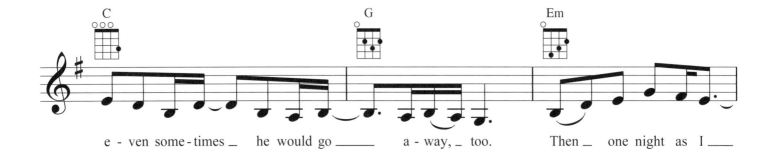

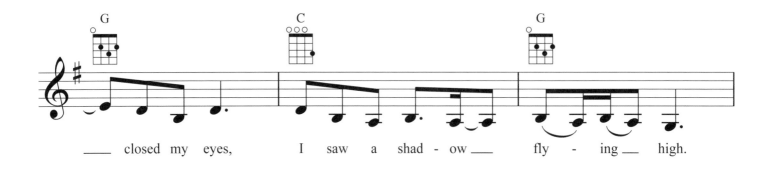

Cap - tain Hook. "Run, run, lost boy," they say to me, _____ "a - way from all of re - al - i - ty." _____ Nev - er - land is home to the lost boys like me; and lost boys like me are ___ free. Nev - er - land is home to the lost boys like me; and

To Coda 1
To Coda 2

Verse

lost boys like me are ___ free. 2. He sprin - kled me in pix - ie dust and

told me to be - lieve, be - lieve _ in him _ and be - lieve in me. "To -

geth - er, we will fly a - way in a cloud of green to _ your beau - ti - ful

des - ti - ny." As we soared a - bove the town that nev - er loved me, I

real - ized I fi - n'lly had a fam - i - ly. Soon e - nough, we reached

Nev - er - land. Peace - ful - ly, my feet hit the sand. And

ev - er since that day...

D.S. al Coda 1

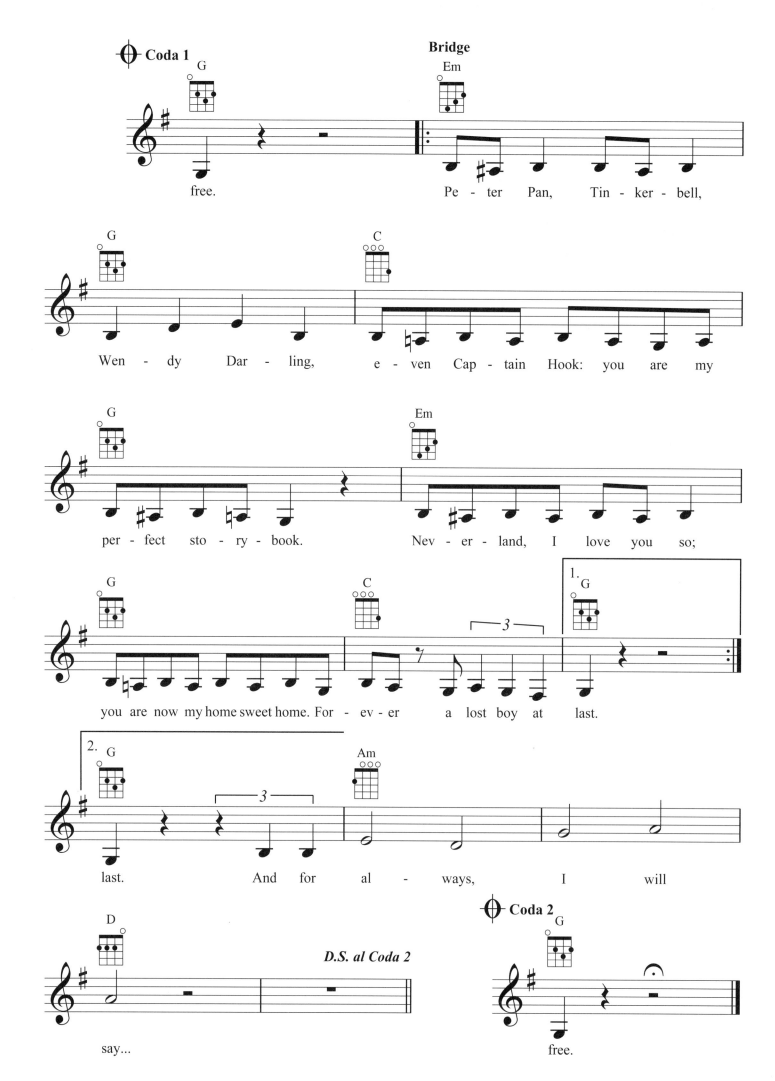

This Is What You Came For

Words and Music by Calvin Harris and Taylor Swift

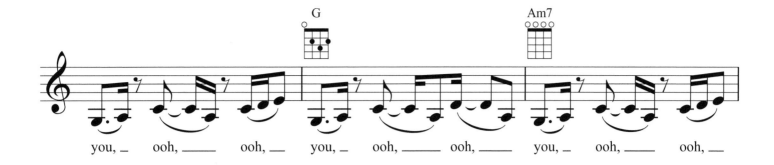

you, _ ooh, ____ ooh, _ you, _ ooh, ____ ooh, ____ you, _ ooh, ____ ooh, __

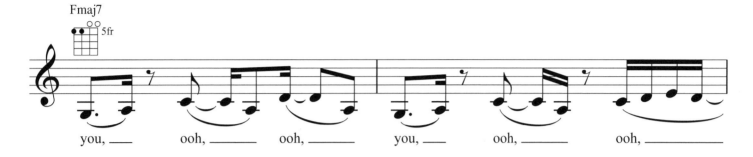

you, ___ ooh, ____ ooh, _____ you, ____ ooh, _____ ooh, _____

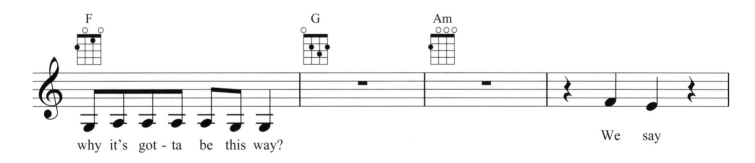

___ ooh. _____   3. We go

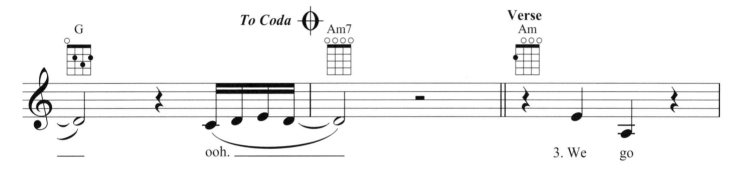

fast with the game we play.   Who knows

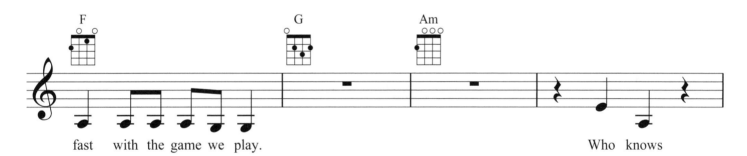

why it's got-ta be this way?   We say

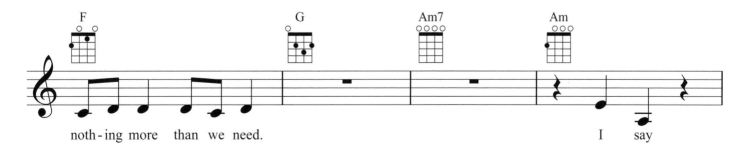

noth-ing more than we need.   I say

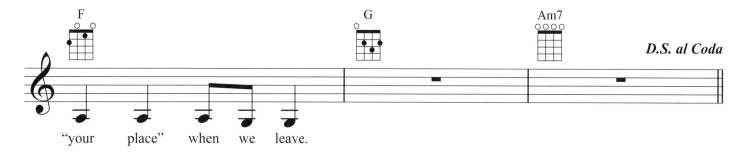

D.S. al Coda

"your place" when we leave.

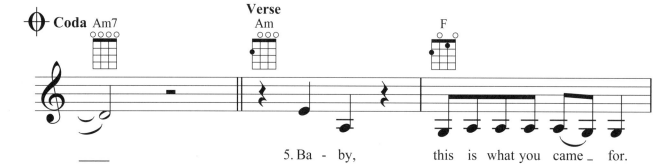

Coda

Verse

5. Ba - by, this is what you came _ for.

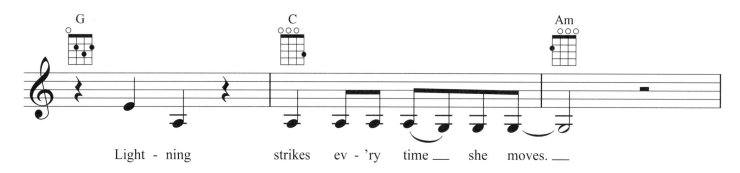

Light - ning strikes ev - 'ry time _ she moves. _

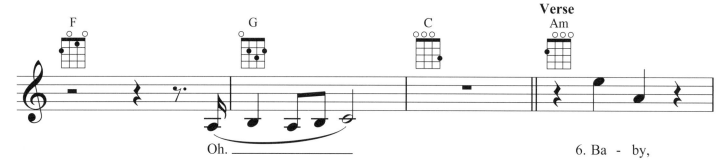

Verse

Oh. _____ 6. Ba - by,

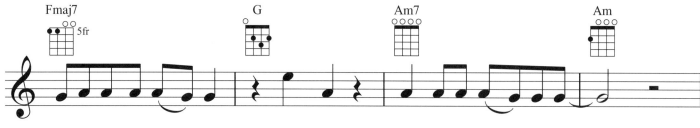

this is what you came _ for. Light - ning strikes ev-'ry time _ she moves. _

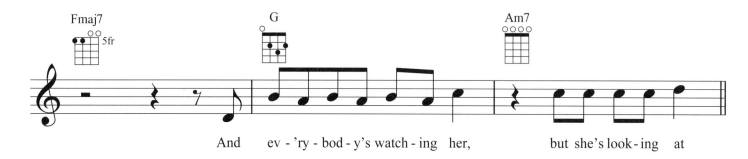

And ev - 'ry - bod - y's watch - ing her, but she's look - ing at

Chorus

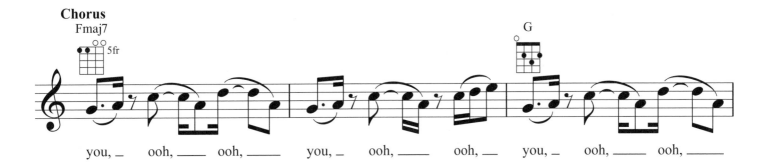

you, __ ooh, ____ ooh, __ you, __ ooh, ____ ooh, __ you, __ ooh, ____ ooh,

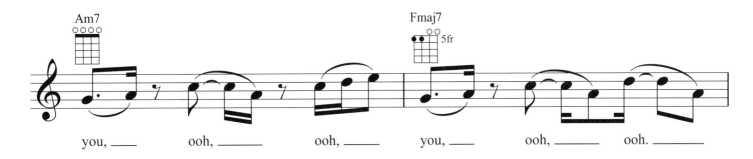

you, ____ ooh, ____ ooh, ____ you, ____ ooh, ____ ooh.

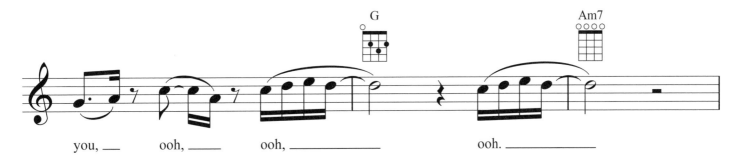

you, __ ooh, ____ ooh, ____ ooh. ____

Outro-Chorus

You, ooh, ____ ooh, ____ you, __ ooh, ____ ooh, __ you, __ ooh, ____ ooh,

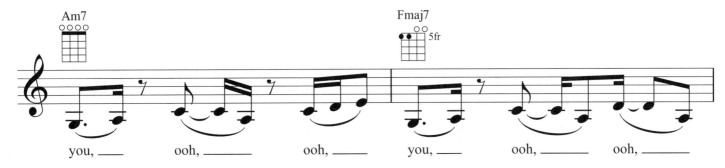

you, ____ ooh, ____ ooh, ____ you, ____ ooh, ____ ooh, ____

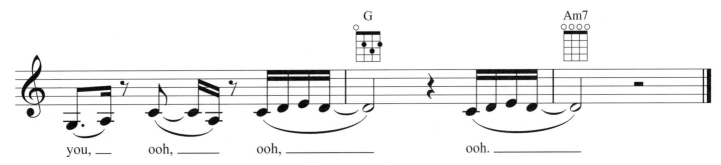

you, __ ooh, ____ ooh, ____ ooh. ____

One Call Away

**Words and Music by Charlie Puth, Breyan Isaac, Matt Prime,
Justin Franks, Blake Anthony Carter and Maureen McDonald**

First note
×× ○ ×

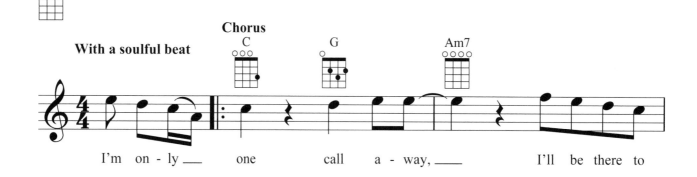

With a soulful beat

Chorus

I'm on-ly ___ one call a-way, ___ I'll be there to

save the day. ___ Su-per-man ___ got ___ noth - ing on me, ___

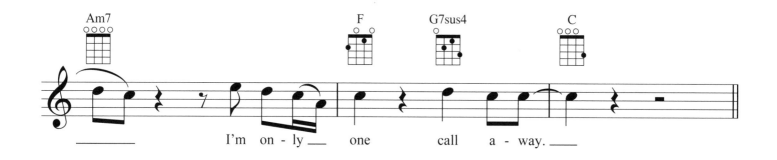

___ I'm on-ly ___ one call a - way. ___

Verse

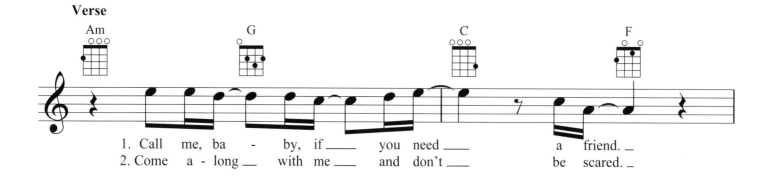

1. Call me, ba - by, if ___ you need ___ a friend. ___
2. Come a - long ___ with me ___ and don't ___ be scared. _

Chorus

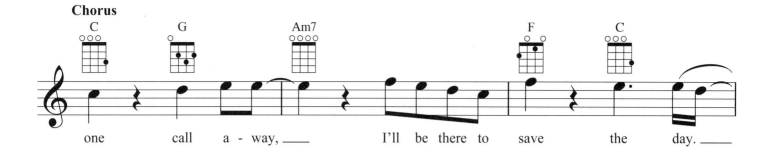

one call a - way, ____ I'll be there to save the day. ____

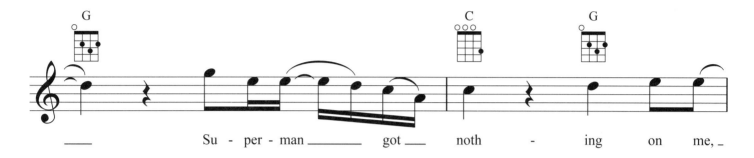

____ Su - per - man ____ got ____ noth - ing on me, __

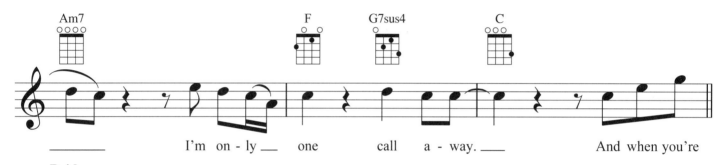

_____ I'm on - ly ___ one call a - way. ___ And when you're

Bridge

weak, I'll be strong. __ I'm gon - na keep hold - ing on. _

_____ Now, don't you wor - ry, it won't be long, ___ dar - ling. When you

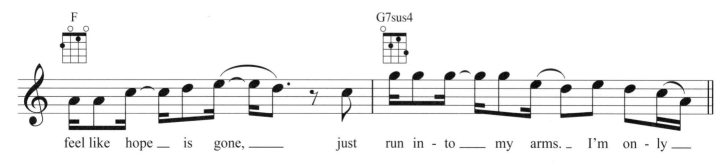

feel like hope __ is gone, ____ just run in - to ___ my arms. __ I'm on - ly __

Chorus

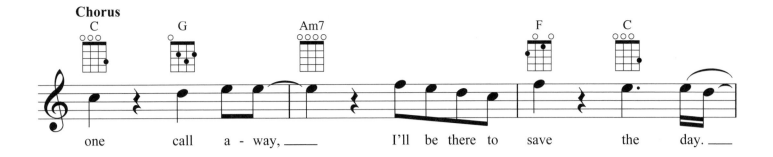

one   call   a - way, _____   I'll be there to   save   the   day. ____

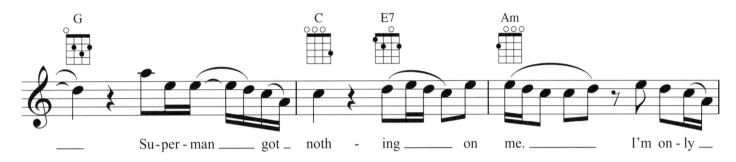

____   Su - per - man _____ got _ noth   -   ing _____ on   me. _____   I'm on - ly _

Outro-Chorus

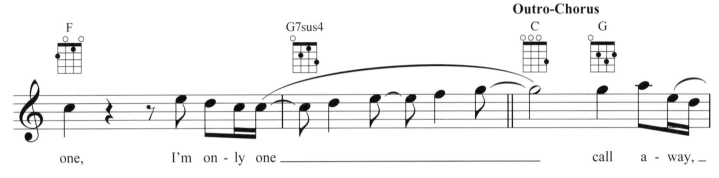

one,   I'm on - ly one _____ call   a - way, _

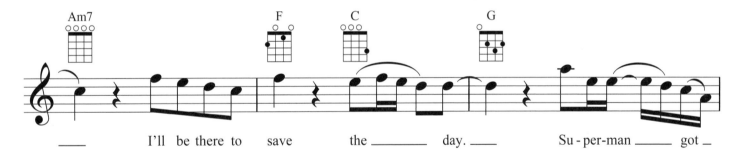

____   I'll be there to   save   the _____ day. ____   Su - per - man _____ got _

noth   -   ing   on   me, _____   I'm on - ly _ one   call   a - way. _

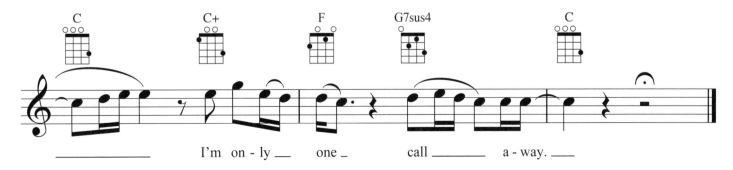

_____   I'm on - ly _ one _ call   a - way. ____

Ophelia

Words and Music by Jeremy Fraites and Wesley Schultz

Verse

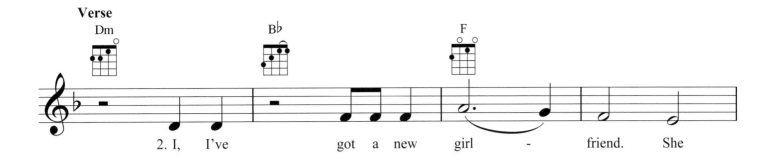

2. I, I've   got a new girl - friend.   She

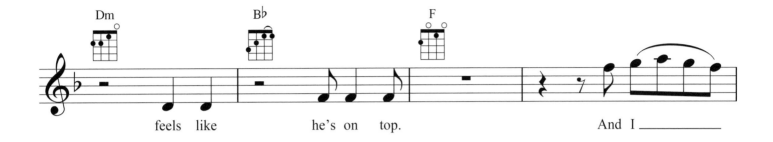

feels like   he's on top.   And I _____

don't feel no re - morse.   And you _____

____ can't see past my blind - ness.

Chorus

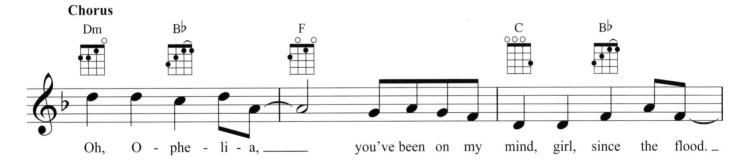

Oh, O - phe - li - a, _____ you've been on my mind, girl, since the flood. _

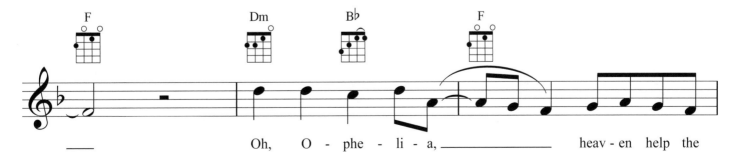

____   Oh, O - phe - li - a, _____ heav - en help the

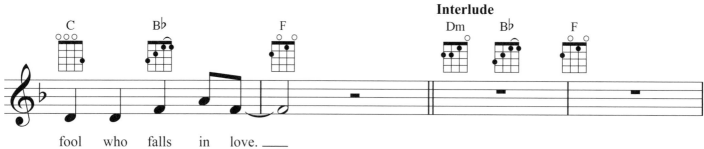

fool who falls in love. ____

Interlude

Verse

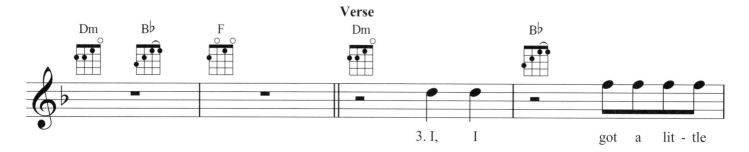

3. I, I got a lit - tle

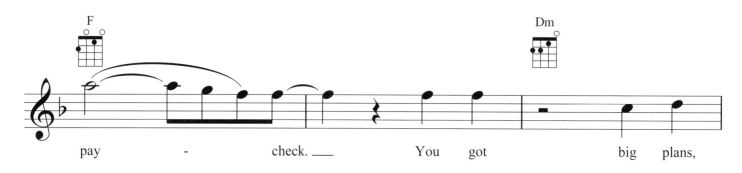

pay - check. ____ You got big plans,

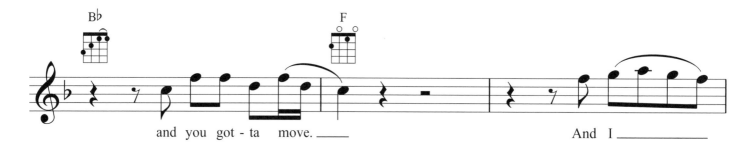

and you got - ta move. ____ And I ____

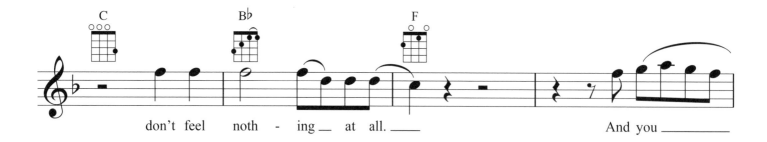

don't feel noth - ing ___ at all. ____ And you ____

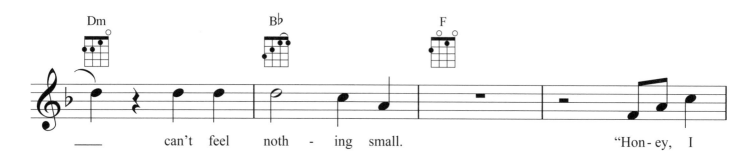

____ can't feel noth - ing small. "Hon - ey, I

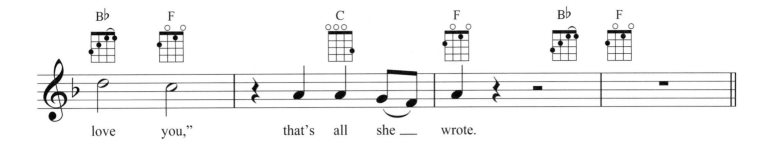

love you," that's all she — wrote.

Chorus

Oh, O - phe - li - a, _____ you've been on my mind, girl, { like a drug. —
{ since the flood. —

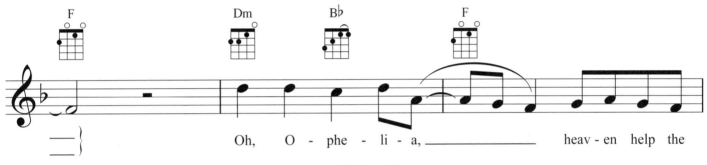

— } Oh, O - phe - li - a, _____ heav - en help the

Outro-Chorus

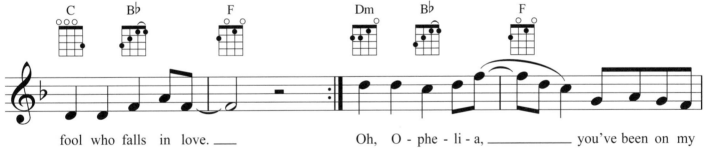

fool who falls in love. ___ Oh, O - phe - li - a, _____ you've been on my

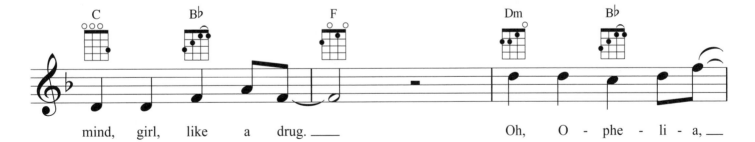

mind, girl, like a drug. ___ Oh, O - phe - li - a, _

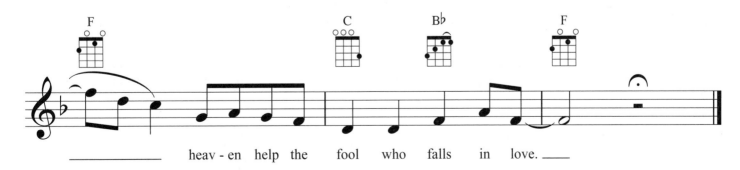

_____ heav - en help the fool who falls in love. ___

7 Years

**Words and Music by Lukas Forchhammer, Morten Ristorp, Stefan Forrest,
David Labrel, Christopher Brown and Morten Pilegaard**

§ **Verse**

Em   D   G   C

2. Once I was e - lev - en years old, my dad - dy told me, "Go get your - self a
3., 5. *See additional lyrics*

D   Em   D   G   Cmaj7

wife or you'll be lone - ly." __ Once I was e - lev - en years old.

Em   D   G

I al - ways had that dream __ like my dad - dy be - fore me,

C   D   Em   D

so I start - ed writ - ing songs, I start - ed writ - ing sto - ries. Some - thing a - bout that glo - ry

G   C   *To Coda* ⊕   D

just al - ways seemed to bore me, 'cause on - ly those I real - ly love will ev - er real - ly know me.

Verse

Em   D   G   C

4. Once I was twen - ty years old, my sto - ry got told, I was writ - ing 'bout ev - 'ry -

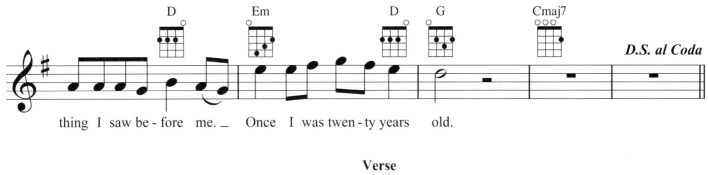

thing I saw be-fore me. _ Once I was twen-ty years old.

Verse

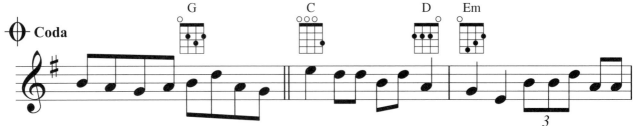

hind. My broth-er, I'm still sor-ry. 6. Soon I'll be six-ty years old. My dad-dy got six-ty-

one. Re-mem-ber life and then your life be-comes a bet-ter one. I made a man so hap-py

when I wrote a let-ter once. I hope my chil-dren come and vis-it once or twice a month.

Soon I'll be six-ty years old. Will I think the world is cold or will I have a lot of

chil-dren who can warm me? _ Soon I'll be six-ty years old.

Additional Lyrics

3. Once I was twenty years old, my story got told
   Before the morning sun, when life was lonely.
   Once I was twenty years old.
   I only see my goals, I don't believe in failure
   'Cause I know the smallest voices, they can make it major.
   I got my boys with me, at least those in favor,
   And if we don't meet before I leave, I hope I'll see you later.

5. Soon we'll be thirty years old. Our songs have been sold,
   We've travelled around the world and we're still roaming.
   Soon we'll be thirty years old.
   I'm still learning about life. My woman brought children for me
   So I can sing them all my songs and I can tell them stories.
   Most of my boys are with me, some are still out seeking glory
   And some I had to leave behind. My brother, I'm still sorry.

Stressed Out

Words and Music by Tyler Joseph

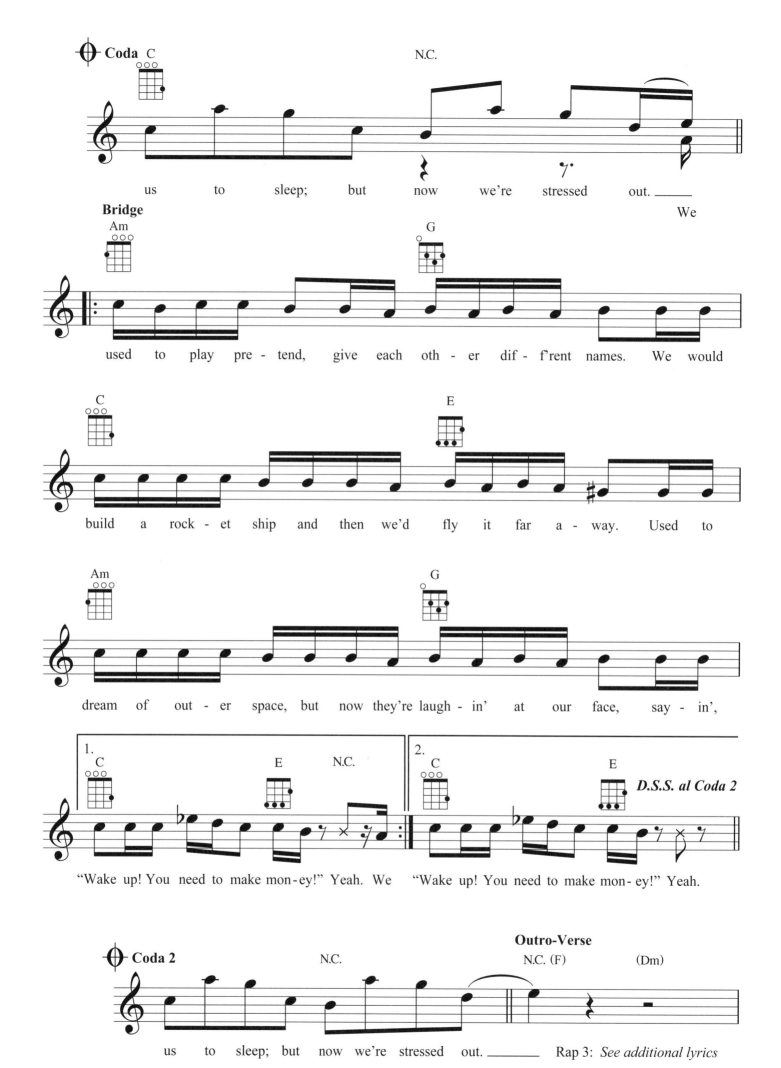

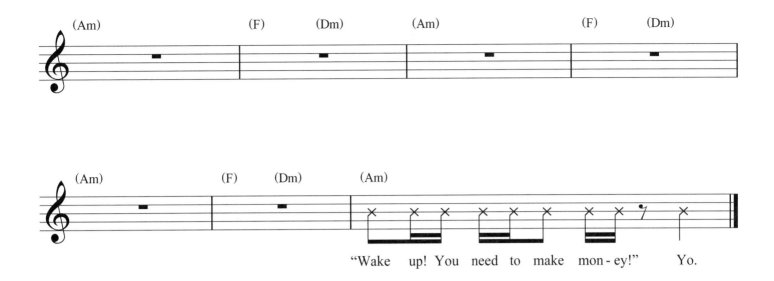

"Wake up! You need to make mon-ey!"   Yo.

Additional Lyrics

Rap 1: I wish I found some better sounds no one's ever heard.
I wish I had a better voice that sang some better words.
I wish I found some chords in an order that is new.
I wish I didn't have to rhyme every time I sang.

I was told when I get older all my fears would shrink,
But now I'm insecure and I care what people think.

Rap 2: Sometimes a certain smell will take me back to when I was young.
How come I'm never able to identify where it's coming from?
I'd make a candle out of it if I ever found it,
Try to sell it, never sell out of it. I'd probably only sell one.

It'd be to my brother, 'cause we have the same nose,
Same clothes, homegrown, a stone's throw from a creek we used to roam.
But it would remind us of when nothing really mattered.
Out of student loans and treehouse homes, we all would take the latter.

Rap 3: We used to play pretend, used to play pretend, bunny.
We used to play pretend; wake up, you need the money.
We used to play pretend, used to play pretend, bunny.
We used to play pretend; wake up, you need the money.

We used to play pretend, give each other different names;
We would build a rocket ship and then we'd fly it far away.
Used to dream of outer space, but now they're laughing at our face,
Saying, "Wake up, you need to make money!" Yo.

Traveller

Words and Music by Chris Stapleton

shirt.   I just ___ keep roll- ing till I'm _____ in the dirt, _

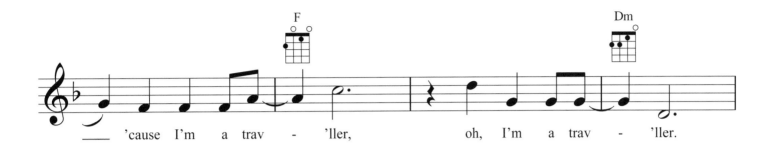

___ 'cause I'm a trav - 'ller,   oh, I'm a trav - 'ller.

I _____ could - n't tell you, hon - ey,   I _____ don't

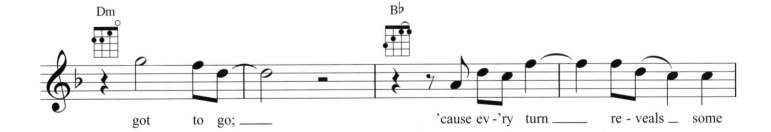

know   where ___ I'm ___ go - ing, but I've

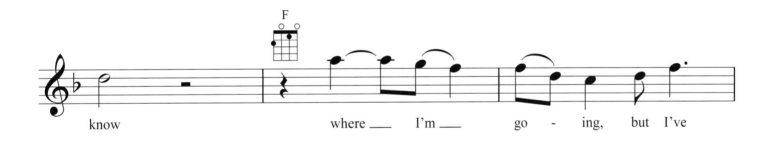

got to go; _____   'cause ev -'ry turn _____ re - veals _ some

oth - er road, _____ and I'm a trav - 'ller,   oh, I'm a trav -

When We Were Young

Words and Music by Adele Adkins and Tobias Jesso Jr.

Pre-Chorus

𝄇 Chorus

_____ it is the last ____ time that ____ we might ____ be ex - act - ly like ____ we were ____

To Coda ⊕

_____ be - fore we re - al - ized ____ we were sad ____ of get - ting old. ____ It made us rest -

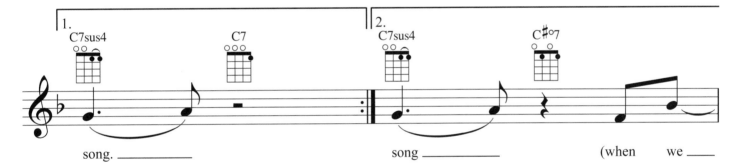

- less. _____ It was just like a mov - ie, it was just like a

song. _____ song _____ (when we ____

_____ were young, ____ when we ____ were young, _____ when we ____

_____ were young, ____ when we ____ were young.) _____ It's hard ____

Bridge

to ad - mit that ev - 'ry - thing __ just takes __ me back __ to when you __

__ were there, __ to when you were there. __ And a part __

__ of me __ keeps hold - ing on, __ just __

__ in case __ it has - n't gone. __ I guess I __ still care. __ Do

Pre-Chorus

you still care? __ It was just like a mov - ie, it was just like a song. __

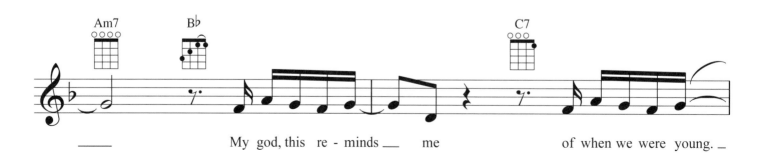

__ My god, this re - minds __ me of when we were young. __

HAL•LEONARD UKULELE PLAY-ALONG®

Now you can play your favorite songs on your uke with great-sounding backing tracks to help you sound like a bona fide pro! The audio also features playback tools so you can adjust the tempo without changing the pitch and loop challenging parts.

1. POP HITS
00701451 Book/CD Pack................$14.99

2. UKE CLASSICS
00701452 Book/CD Pack................$12.99

3. HAWAIIAN FAVORITES
00701453 Book/CD Pack................$12.99

4. CHILDREN'S SONGS
00701454 Book/CD Pack................$12.99

5. CHRISTMAS SONGS
00701696 Book/CD Pack................$12.99

6. LENNON & MCCARTNEY
00701723 Book/CD Pack................$12.99

7. DISNEY FAVORITES
00701724 Book/CD Pack................$12.99

8. CHART HITS
00701745 Book/CD Pack................$14.99

9. THE SOUND OF MUSIC
00701784 Book/CD Pack................$12.99

10. MOTOWN
00701964 Book/CD Pack................$12.99

11. CHRISTMAS STRUMMING
00702458 Book/CD Pack................$12.99

12. BLUEGRASS FAVORITES
00702584 Book/CD Pack................$12.99

13. UKULELE SONGS
00702599 Book/CD Pack................$12.99

14. JOHNNY CASH
00702615 Book/CD Pack................$14.99

15. COUNTRY CLASSICS
00702834 Book/CD Pack................$12.99

16. STANDARDS
00702835 Book/CD Pack................$12.99

17. POP STANDARDS
00702836 Book/CD Pack................$12.99

18. IRISH SONGS
00703086 Book/CD Pack................$12.99

19. BLUES STANDARDS
00703087 Book/CD Pack................$12.99

20. FOLK POP ROCK
00703088 Book/CD Pack................$12.99

21. HAWAIIAN CLASSICS
00703097 Book/CD Pack................$12.99

22. ISLAND SONGS
00703098 Book/CD Pack................$12.99

23. TAYLOR SWIFT
00704106 Book/CD Pack................$14.99

24. WINTER WONDERLAND
00101871 Book/CD Pack................$12.99

25. GREEN DAY
00110398 Book/CD Pack................$14.99

26. BOB MARLEY
00110399 Book/CD Pack................$14.99

27. TIN PAN ALLEY
00116358 Book/CD Pack................$12.99

28. STEVIE WONDER
00116736 Book/CD Pack................$14.99

29. OVER THE RAINBOW & OTHER FAVORITES
00117076 Book/CD Pack................$14.99

30. ACOUSTIC SONGS
00122336 Book/CD Pack................$14.99

31. JASON MRAZ
00124166 Book/CD Pack................$14.99

32. TOP DOWNLOADS
00127507 Book/CD Pack................$14.99

33. CLASSICAL THEMES
00127892 Book/Online Audio..........$14.99

34. CHRISTMAS HITS
00128602 Book/CD Pack................$14.99

35. SONGS FOR BEGINNERS
00129009 Book/Online Audio..........$14.99

36. ELVIS PRESLEY HAWAII
00138199 Book/CD Pack................$14.99

39. GYPSY JAZZ
00146559 Book/Online Audio..........$14.99

HAL•LEONARD® CORPORATION

7777 W. BLUEMOUND RD. P.O. BOX 13819 MILWAUKEE, WI 53213

www.halleonard.com

Prices, contents, and availability
subject to change without notice.

0616